The Modern Al_ Authentic Principles to Become the Man You Were Born to Be… and Attract Women, Win Friends, Increase Confidence, Gain Charisma, Master Leadership, and Dominate Life

By Patrick King
Dating and Social Skills Coach at
www.PatrickKingConsulting.com

The Modern Alpha Male: Authentic Principles to Become the Man You Were Born to Be… and Attract Women, Win Friends, Increase Confidence, Gain Charisma, Master Leadership, and Dominate Life

Introduction

1. Alpha males prioritize personal growth and don't settle for the status quo.

2. Alpha males have supreme confidence and security in themselves.

3. Alpha males are always composed and in control of the situation.

4. Alpha males look their fears in the eye and laugh at them.

5. Alpha males assume responsibility.

6. Alpha males have self-knowledge that inspire their true confidence.

7. Alpha males give women the respect they deserve.

8. Alpha males are natural leaders because of how they treat others.

9. Alpha males find joy in their journey.

10. Alpha males don't mind taking the road less traveled.

11. Alpha males are self-reliant and independent.

12. Alpha males respect themselves enough to be in great shape.

13. Alpha males embrace role models.

14. Alpha males embrace vulnerability.

15. The 28 day Alpha Male Kickstart Plan.

Conclusion

Cheat sheet

Introduction

I want to get this out of the way immediately.

Everything you think you know about alpha males, toss it out the window. It's outdated, chauvinistic, or just plain wrong.

And it's not even your fault. Just think about how we're conditioned to think about an alpha male by our media and society.

He's the cock of the walk that is assertive and takes charge of any situation. He's extroverted, amazingly social and friendly, and has an amazing group of friends. He gets as many women as he can schedule into his calendar, which is also packed with hobbies and passions that he excels at. He lights up any room that he enters and has a serious case of charm and magnetism.

What about…

He's a dominating shark, and excels at intimidating his opponents into the ground. He verges on being overly aggressive even with his friends, and tends to offend people consistently. He has anger issues and is no stranger to bar fights. However, he comes to your defense immediately if you're ever down and out, and will march with you to hell and back.

Either of those descriptions conjure up a crystal clear image of someone fictional that is their epitome. Okay, so there's a major problem with this.

Do either of those descriptions reflect reality? Specifically, do they reflect **your authentic reality**? Is that your conception of the alpha male, and does that fit within your authentic personality?

Let's be clear here, it's not a matter of polishing a turd. You're so much more than you give yourself credit for. But sometimes we can try all we want, and the square peg won't fit into the circle hole.

And there's nothing wrong with that. That doesn't mean that you can't be an alpha male… and that's also why I have named my book The <u>Modern</u> Alpha Male.

It's not about fitting into people's pre-conceptions of what an alpha male entails. You're just pretending to be somebody else in that instance, and that's building your castle on quicksand. Your identity will be false, and so will all the beliefs that it is based on. The best you'll ever be is a pale imitation of a concept of a man... and that is a lot of degrees of separation from where we want to truly be.

Instead of posing as an alpha male, it's a matter of learning to embody a host of the authentic traits that I describe within. Your castle will be built upon solid bedrock, and the walls will be unscaleable because after time, it will be your true identity.

As my book title promises, you will absolutely attract women, win friends, increase confidence, gain charisma, and master leadership when you first learn to work on yourself and bulletproof your inner confidence and self-worth.

Becoming the modern alpha male is about calibrating a host of positive traits to your own personality and using them together to take your mindset and approach to life to new heights. The emphasis here should be on how each person calibrates to their **own** version and conception of a modern alpha male, with everyone being correct in their own right.

That's the essence of the modern alpha male. He is self-assured in his own identity to forge his own path to the best version of himself... which is really what the alpha male stands for. He seeks to grow himself to the best authentic version of himself. Squeeze every bit of your personal potential out and

It sounds like a tall task, but there's good news waiting. The modern alpha male... the best version of yourself... these are all learned habits, traits, and behaviors. They weren't just programmed in some people's genes and simply lacking in yours like in the movie GATTACA.

Amazing, positive personality traits aren't just handed out in the biological lottery.

It's your choice to master them and become the man you were born to be.

Seize it now.

1. Alpha males prioritize personal growth and don't settle for the status quo.

Ever heard the myth that if a shark stops swimming, he sinks to the bottom of the ocean? He's as good as dead.

An alpha male embodies exactly the same mentality. He's a shark and he knows it. He seizes what he wants and takes as direct a path to it as socially possible.

More importantly an alpha male knows that if he stops swimming – improving himself and growing personally – then he is as dead as that shark at the bottom of your aquarium. (Shark in your aquarium?! That's pretty damn luxurious.)

True alpha males know that they are perpetual works in progress, which is a mindset that is both humbling and empowering. They won't be great at everything, but they can and will get there someday.

They know that life is a journey and a process, and the status quo should never represent satisfaction to them. There is never really a point in anyone's life when someone becomes complete and arrives, like a butterfly out of a cocoon. There are always rough spots that even the butterfly must weather, be it in their personal life, their professional life, academically, intellectually... the list goes on.

Rough spots and challenges indicate the need and opportunity for growth, and that is why alpha males always rise to the challenge and seek to take something from each experience that will make them a more developed alpha male... but they will always be trying to complete themselves.

It's a process of never-ending education that you simply don't learn in school, books, or formal classes. Self-development comes from an intentional purpose-driven mindset of improving and maturing – travel, meeting new people, and overcoming challenges are the hallmark of that.

Alpha males don't shrink away in fear or feel that they are lucky to simply hang on to what they currently have. They strive to grow by learning to cope, and know that new perspectives are more valuable than most of the classes they took in school. Come on, how often do you have to find a calculus derivative past age 20?

Change is usually difficult, but it's not always negative – the alpha male welcomes change because they know that change is the only constant in life. They can choose to embrace it and improve with it, or be dragged by it kicking and screaming. You tell me which way is optimal.

New people, new careers, new situations, new homes – these are all challenges to overcome, and aren't necessarily negative at all.

Personal growth is also highly assisted by being goal-oriented. Alpha males realize that optimal growth requires intentionality and direction, so they commit to short-term, intermediate, and long-term goals for every aspect of their lives. Alpha males are people who are going places in life, and understand that their energy must be used in an efficient and focused manner to truly improve.

Goals can exist in every aspect of an alpha male's life: money, career, education, love, relationships, and family. Alpha males don't float with any of these important areas of life, and they don't drift and waste their energy running around in circles. Their calendars are regimented and detailed beasts, and aren't just for marking brunch dates with their parents.

For each goal, an alpha male will break it down into major objectives, sub-goals, and daily to-do lists in the name of self-development and improvement. This focus provides direction and organizes energy which would otherwise be spent goofing off or on Netflix. They see meaning in everything that they do, and they only engage in actions that are focused and have meaning.

Unsurprisingly, they are usually able to accomplish far more than the people around them because of this intentional focus in pursuit of growth.

Real alpha males have goals and prioritize personal growth. This also means that they will never settle for less than they set their minds out for. They never make excuses, because they know that as long as their goals are clear, their constant focus and have will propel them to victory.

Settling is never an option. Just good enough is not good enough, and any improvement is only a step towards the ultimate goal – this is why an alpha male's goals are sky-high, even for his 1, 3, 5, and 10 year timelines.

Having a goal gives you a clear idea of what you want, how you simply cannot settle for less, and how exactly you can improve yourself in areas of personal growth and development.

Be the alpha shark that never stops swimming and rule the ocean.

2. Alpha males have supreme confidence and security in themselves.

If you ask anyone if they think they are independent and have their own strong identity, chances are that 99% of people are going to emphatically agree with that statement.

That's too bad, because deep down inside, 99% of people are really herd animals.

They go with the crowd, follow the herd mentality, avoid sticking out, and most importantly, let others influence their opinions and how they go about their lives. It's not their fault; it's easy to fall into group think, and it's often the path of least resistance because you won't have to overcome challenges that way.

Besides being the easiest path of life, there are also many reasons why people tend to stick to group thinking and not deviate from the norm. You can even trace it back to our evolutionary roots.

Thousands of years ago, our ancestors HAD to stay with the pack because there was safety in numbers, and if they strayed they might find themselves instantly devoured by a saber-toothed tiger. There was actual value in group thinking, and individuals who tried to forge their own path simply weren't likely to pass their genes on.

This amazingly strong group instinct was so strong and salient that it is still seared into our subconscious, and informs many of our daily actions. However, instead of there being actual negative consequences such as being torn apart by a vicious predator, now all we have to deal with is social and peer pressure. Peer pressure isn't always easy to resist, so it takes some serious strength of character to break out of our herd mentality comfort zone.

But guess what: modern living no longer rewards those who only stick with the herd. Modern living rewards those who are able to break free of group think because we're no longer stalking the savannah in search of a gazelle to hunt. If you can't think outside of conventional wisdom these days, it simply means that your ideas and actions are doomed to mediocrity. We live in a fast-changing world that rewards innovation, and you just aren't going to cut it.

The alpha male isn't afraid of offending others by sticking out of the herd, and is unapologetic with who he is. Some may hate him, but more will love him for this, and he's not trying to please everyone. This lets him find his true friends and tribe quickly as like attracts like.

Guess what alpha males do?

They blaze their own damn trail and follow the path that they want, regardless of whether it's the path less taken, or never taken. They aren't afraid of sticking out from the group, and realize that falling in with the rest of the group is simply average. That's just not acceptable.

Alpha males strive for more, hunger for more, and usually attain it.

And guess why they feel comfortable doing this?

Alpha males have a powerful sense of their personal identity.

When you are confident and comfortable with who you are, your abilities and your limitations, you know deep inside what you want your path to be. And that confidence tells you that it's a damned good path to be pursuing, so you can't help but pursue it.

Unsurprisingly, these traits of character and confidence are ones that people typically find extremely attractive and magnetic — one of the many ways that an alpha male is not a strong male, but a charismatic leader.

The key to all self-confidence and security in oneself boils down to one singular aspect: respect for themselves and others.

It takes a high level of self-respect to follow your own path because your own investigation and your own thinking has led you there. You just don't respect yourself if you automatically push aside your own ideas, your own thinking, and your own views and adopt others' views.

There is no healthy self-respect here. You are simply going along a path set for you by others.

Similarly, alpha males are able to take an independent stand precisely because they respect other people's ideas enough to challenge it. They look at the conclusions others have come to and they review it based on their own experiences and observations. Alpha males don't automatically assume conventional wisdom is correct. They respect the ideas of others enough to give those ideas the review, the scrutiny, and the challenges they deserve.

You don't oppose just to oppose. Instead, you respectfully add to people's body of knowledge by carefully lining up common held beliefs against your perception and lived experience.

Alpha males don't believe something just because it was handed to them. Instead, they respect their own ability to come to their conclusion and judge personal truths. This is why they are independent thinkers and always line up whatever accepted belief against what they see, hear, smell, touch, feel, and taste.

This is the foundation of real self-confidence and leadership.

3. Alpha males are always composed and in control of the situation.

An alpha male is as even-keeled as they come, and is always in control of his emotions. He knows that losing control is a sign of weakness and though he expresses his emotions without fail, he never allows them to consume him and cloud his judgment.

He is a cool cucumber, and this ability allows him to be the leader in many situations, and stand above the pack in others.

Picture the following situation that the cool, composed alpha male might handle differently from others: you've walked out of your office building to see your new car's rear bumper smashed in and hanging to the ground by an invisible hit and run asshole.

How do you react? Do you get angry and start screaming? Do you begin imagining the medieval torture techniques you'd like to subject the asshole drive to?

Or do you take a deep breath, bite your lip, take pictures, and call your insurance company immediately?

Guess which path the alpha male takes? He remains calm and refuses to let any situation own him. And guess which approach gets a better result with the insurance company and dealing with the asshole driver's aftermath?

There is a very simple secret as to why alpha males always seem to be in control of the situation, and why they always seem to make the right decisions to produce the best results.

Ready for it? Here it is.

Alpha males realize that they cannot always control the situation… but they can always control their response to them. The world will throw us curveballs on a daily basis, and there's nothing we can do about it. But controlling their reactions and emotions enable them to make the right decision repeatedly while others would flip out in the same position. This emotional control puts their fate and destiny sole in their hands, and this mindset is exactly why alpha males win and dominate.

Let's dig deeper into this. The inconvenient truth is that life is random, life takes sharp turns, and life is impossible to truly control. So the alpha male controls what he can: his response and reactions. Remaining calm and composed is a high-value reaction, and the alpha male knows it.

To master and dominate the world, the alpha male knows that he must master himself first. Controlling your calm and cool keeps outcomes within you're your control, as opposed to panic, rage, or recoiling in fear, you gather information, weigh different possibilities, and keep a clear mind as to your next three steps. You think about how your choice can impact not just yourself but other people as well.

This ability and introspection is what separates effective leaders and alpha males who make strong and informed decisions… from weak and ineffective leaders who let their emotions overwhelm and overcome them.

Weak people make weak decisions purely out of emotion and then backtrack to rationalize their decisions. We have all seen this happen. They'll try to justify their 'heat of the moment' choices with reasons they only thought of before to make themselves appear decisive and justified.

It's a long process that leads one to embrace this inner calm and strength, but it starts with believing your intuition and trusting in your values. When you have confidence in your values, combined with inner calm, you'll be able to make alpha decisions from a position of confident strength. Best of all, carrying yourself this way reassures people around you and makes you a strong, unquestionable leader.

An alpha male's decisiveness flows from an inner reserve of calm strength and conviction after a fact-based process. When people aren't operating from an inner sense of calm, they are easily sidetracked by opinion. They confuse their prejudices for truth. They mistake their biases for fact. Alpha males are able to keep their emotions at arm's length so they can see the full picture. Instead of taking shots in the dark, they take aimed, measured steps that go a long way in resolving problems the right way.

If you want to become an alpha male, the first step you can take is to start thinking like one. Begin by understanding that your inner world reflects your outer world. If you want to be in control, wealthy, powerful, driven, and effective, you need to control your emotions and operate from a strong sense of inner calm. Few people are able to do this but the good news is thinking like this is a choice. Are you ready to make progress with your life or continue to make excuses? It is your choice.

4. Alpha males look their fears in the eye and laugh at them.

As I have hinted to throughout this book thus far, an alpha male is no different from any other male, really. They just possess a series of mindsets and perspectives about themselves and the world that give them character and strength.

A big piece of that is the willingness to look into the eye of his worst fears and laugh at them. He might be faking it, he might be insane, and he might not truly believe he can do it. But the important part is taking a stand against his fears, making a leap of faith to conquer them, and becoming a far stronger man because of it.

The true alpha male knows that his fears are not always rational, and the consequences of failure are never really that bad… so there is rarely a good reason to not confront a fear. The alternative will never be as bad as he imagines, and might contain numerous silver linings.

The allure and admiration for conquering fears is part of the reason that we all have different heroes that we all look up to. We love and admire them because they embody qualities and traits that we wish we possessed. Undoubtedly, it's also an element of envy that they have truly accomplished something that we might be too afraid to even attempt to.

Did these alpha male role models set out to conquer their fears?

Maybe, and maybe not.

I'll tell you what was more integral to their success, however: a willingness to reach for their goals no matter the cost, obstacles, or fears in their way.

It's not always simple bravery that alpha males possess. Alpha males have fears too, and get as scared as the rest of us. But they often have an insatiable drive to accomplish goals that takes them out of their comfort zone and to the limits of their courage.

In other words, courage doesn't have to outright and blatant courage itself; sometimes the pursuit and focus on a goal is enough to overcome obstacles that we wouldn't otherwise.

You need to develop this alpha male habit by knowing exactly what outcome you want from any situation, and make it an explicit goal.

At a party, do you want to get phone numbers or talk to strangers? At a networking event, maybe you want to collect 20 business cards? And so on.

Once you know what you want, enter the mindset that nothing will get in your way in order to achieve it. Treat that like a crutch if you need to—for alpha males, this comes naturally with time.

And what about conquering your fears? What if in order to finish that marathon, you need to train for a long time, and you don't think you could survive that process? Or you get nervous when talking to strangers?

This is where the drive to complete goals overrides your fear. Alphas may be afraid, but the end goal is more important.

It's not supposed to be easy to be an alpha male, or else everyone would be doing it. You're probably going to have to practice keeping your end goal in mind, and having that supersede all your current fears.

Hell, if you were a new surgeon and you had to do an emergency heart transplant... you'd put your fears aside in pursuit of the end goal of saving a life, wouldn't you?

You'll have to practice. Scared of talking to people? Go to bars where messing up won't matter, or talk to cashiers incessantly. Go on a lot of dates until talking to a woman comes naturally.

It doesn't matter if you do poorly in the beginning, it just matters that you try and get used to facing that particular fear. Scared of pushing yourself physically? Make tiny goals, and start at a pace or a number you already know you can achieve.

The key to making sure you are successful is by already knowing your limits, and being honest as to how far away from them you are. Alpha males always see the limits, but their mindset keeps them from giving up.

Alpha males always learn from their fears, especially the times when they don't succeed at conquering them. Alpha males take that new knowledge and use it to make the next attempt better.

A failure isn't something to be regret, it's a gifted opportunity for improvement.

5. Alpha males assume responsibility.

If you've ever had co-workers in your life, you'll have someone in mind when you read the following description.

A co-worker who is his own loudest cheerleader and loves telling people about that one time he succeeded, pulled in a new account, won someone over... and yet is completely silent in his losses and when he's wrong.

To top it off, he's got an amazingly punch-able face.

These people are rarely leaders for numerous reasons... but mostly because they lack the sense of true responsibility that an ideal leader must possess in all of his actions.

It's one of the most powerful traits that makes us want to rally behind and follow someone to hell and back. A person that takes responsibility for their actions (and those that they lead) is a signal of true confidence and power.

Part of this mindset is also being willing to take charge, which an alpha male is comfortable and even used to. If he can pre-empt a bad situation and fix it, he will happily take that burden on as well.

Alpha males know the proper way to take responsibility for their actions, especially when a situation has taken a turn for the worse. It's a mindset that follows alpha males everywhere.

Taking responsibility for your actions comes in three major parts. Alpha males think about others before themselves, and so this process happens naturally and instantly. Honor and courage are things that are instilled in their personality, so most of the time, they don't even realize the process that I'm going to lay out below.

Admitting what you did wrong.

This is often the hardest part. People's egos get in the way of their clarity, and they will often blame others around them for something that was either partially or entirely their fault. People don't like admitting that they are at fault, as it is sometimes embarrassing. Even if others are to blame, admit what you did to create the current situation. Be specific, and be respectful.

Apologize for what you did.

Sometimes just telling someone you were wrong, and that you're sorry is enough to fix the situation. Apologies show humbleness, and humility is the first sign of a strong, healthy self-esteem. Be the first to act and speak out. When you apologize, make sure you mean it. People can always tell when you're lying.

Tell the person or people involved how you plan on fixing it.

This could be as simple as, "I promise to never do this again," or as complicated as, "I will pay for your window to be replaced, and also wash all the others on that floor of your house." Why is this important? Because after acknowledging you've done something wrong, making it up to the person shows that you realize you hurt their feelings and you'd like to fix that. It shows a deep sensitivity and an honor few people possess.

Alpha males learn from every situation. They're always trying to be better, and when something fails, they look at all the ways to never have that happen again. Make sure to treat each failed situation as a learning experience, and then change your path, even if it means asking for the opinions or help of others.

Alphas know asking for help isn't a sign of weakness, but a sign of wisdom.

6. Alpha males have self-knowledge that inspire their true confidence.

One of the greatest misconceptions about the alpha male is that they are strong because of their social stature, how others regard them, or the validation that they constantly receive from other people.

This is incredibly wrong.

They do get all of those things, but every single benefit that the alpha male enjoys is because of how they view their strengths and weaknesses, which allows him to project a true confidence and vulnerability whenever each is appropriate.

His strength comes from the inside, and so do all of the benefits.

This is a powerful truth that I can never repeat enough – if you draw your strength from circumstances and other people, both outside of your control, you will forever be at the mercy of those circumstances and people.

It's a cycle of uncertainty that ultimately is very unsatisfying and dangerous to revolve around. You're building a house of cards that can crumble at any second. You have no foundation, and you are weak from the inside to out.

Alpha males have their own independent source of strength. They are just comfortable in their own skin, and realize that no one is perfect. They know themselves. They embrace their flaws, while simultaneously trying to improve upon them. They are okay with being vulnerable and know that vulnerability inspires true strength.

They aren't trying to be something they are not, and they aren't trying to prove themselves to others constantly.

And guess what? I've also just described an extremely attractive male that will draw people to him. A charismatic leader that others will enjoy following.

When somebody truly knows himself and knows his limits… this is the big difference between being cocky, putting on a show, or trying to be something that you're not… and being real.

A real alpha male is all about authenticity. In fact, he is the first one to acknowledge his shortcomings. This is why he never comes off as arrogant or smug.

Alpha males understand that seeking validation from others is weakness. He doesn't define his value based on others' estimation. He has his own core set of values. As long as he lives his life based on a strong sense of integrity, he is happy, and that is one source of strength the world cannot take away from him.

This is precisely why alpha males are so confident. He respects others but respects himself enough not to mimic or ape others.

This is also why alpha males are not afraid of rejection. They understand the differences among people and respect those differences. Just because a female isn't attracted doesn't destroy him because he doesn't define himself based on other people's validation.

If you draw your confidence from what other people think about you, you will never find lasting happiness or your own strength. Let your self-knowledge about your strengths and weaknesses guide your confidence to new heights.

View your confidence as suit of armor that you've had since you were a child. It protects your psyche and ego, but definitely has weak spots. However, the weak spots and dents in the armor are what make you uniquely you.

A perfectly unharmed suit of armor is either fake... or untested. You're tested and you've weathered the storm and come out surviving and thriving. Nothing is going to kill you, and people can see that. Wear that armor proudly!

7. Alpha males give women the respect they deserve.

The sad reality of modern western society is that men are not trained to respect women.

The stereotypical alpha male doesn't take care of women, he merely uses them as an object for his own pleasure. Let's be real this is likely one of your goals by reading books like this. It's certainly possible, but the true alpha male doesn't just use women for their bodies.

He cherishes them for who they are, who they aspire to be, their hopes and dreams, their insecurities and flaws, how they choose to present themselves to the world, and generally gives them the respect that anyone deserves.

Women aren't just for alpha males to dominate and use to show dominance. Respect should never be situational, and is the foundation of attraction.

Other guys play games to manipulate women or to exploit the insecurities and weaknesses of women. That's bullshit.

We know that it undoubtedly works sometimes, but at what cost? To have successfully manipulated someone into your bed in a very hollow victory, and speaks volumes about the negative intentions those types of men carry around with them on a daily basis. They are not men; they are pussies.

Real attraction that leads to real, meaningful relationships doesn't involve any of that bullshit. It doesn't involve manipulation or exploitation.

Real respect for women is about accepting yourself, which alpha males embody, and above all else, accepting her for who she is and seeing her as a person with her own thoughts and feelings. This means a fundamental appreciation of the fact that you're both imperfect and that is perfectly okay.

Unfortunately, we live in a society where we have heaps of expectations and entitlements about the women that we want. We have a laundry list of traits and requirements for them. This is counterproductive in so many ways, but primarily that whenever expectations pop up, it means that reality will be that much more unsatisfying and difficult to obtain. Throughout this jumble, it is no surprise that most people that played the dating game are often frustrated, desperate, and essentially feel empty.

The alpha male stands apart from this. His foundation in attracting women is rooted in respect and honesty.

Think about it. There is really no respect if you have to lie for others to like you. Real respect is based on knowing your imperfections and liking each other despite them, being honest with who you really are, and having no illusions about other people to put your head and shoulders above everybody else.

Yes, this might mean you might have less dates but those would be real dates. Those would be dates that may lead to real relationships based on a real understanding and appreciation of each other. A relationship based on a lie is not a real relationship.

Alpha males rarely land in the friend zone because of this fundamental truth. They base their relationships on real respect. They are transparent with their feelings and intentions. What you see is what you get. No hiding, tricks, or games. If they have sexual intentions, they don't hide them and confidently express themselves.

They respect their potential partner, and this is why they don't try to remake that other person. They don't try to extract from them or leech from them some sort of personality flaw that they themselves are missing. They don't look at their partners as some sort of psychotherapeutic device that would complete them. They are not users.

This is what separates real alpha males from guys who are faking it. Their relationships allow both partners to speak their mind and to be open with each other regarding their intentions. Their relationships allow both partners to see eye to eye on a deep level.

With such transparent intentions, no wonder alpha males are strangers to the friend zone.

8. Alpha males are natural leaders because of how they treat others.

Modern society has socially conditioned us in some peculiar ways.

One of the most interesting and not necessarily positive ways is that we are fake to others on a daily basis.

We have fake friendships, relationships, and even love affairs. People are fake in general, and mostly this is not intentional.

For the most part, people tolerate this. For the most part, people settle for this.

This is not something the alpha male tolerates, and this is a part of what makes him an amazing and natural leader. They are incredibly authentic in their actions and how they relate and treat other people.

They impart **infectious confidence**, and that, above anything that Machiavelli proposes, is the key to being a charismatic leader.

Infectious confidence is given by appreciating others, publicly, often, loudly, and early.

This is not a new concept, as any leadership book will advise you to praise in public and criticize in private, or some variation of positivity.

The problem with that advice is that it's missing the most important part – authenticity. Authentic appreciation is the key to imparting your infectious confidence, and

Alpha males make for great leaders because their appreciation is honest. They don't fake it. They base their appreciation on actual evidence of competence in their underlings and the people around them. This makes their compliments and appreciation even more valuable. You have to remember, appreciation just like candy loses its value when you hand it out all the time.

Another reason why alpha males are truly respected and their leadership valued is because they show appreciation not because they're looking for something in return, or because they feel forced to show appreciation because "that's what leaders do."

The genuineness is what sets their appreciation and compliments apart from fake leaders. This is why subordinates grow to love them, and will go above and beyond for them.

When you show that you are supremely confident in them, it will build up their own confidence… and they will remember that you helped them reach that point. It's a powerful effect that benefits you to no end.

This also speaks to the conviction that a true alpha male leader must have, and pass down to those that he ends up leading.

Alpha males mean what they say and say what they mean. They are never hypocrites, and they are very decisive.

A precursor to imparting all of these amazingly positive feelings is respect and knowledge for yourself. You have to know your limitations, you have to know your capabilities, and you have to respect your capacity for leadership.

It is this self-knowledge that really cements the alpha male's natural leadership. They may not have the title. They may not be high up on the hierarchy, but the way their self-respect and self-knowledge manifest itself in their lives makes them natural leaders and magnets to be followed.

Not surprisingly, they eventually move up the hierarchy because people are drawn to confident people. People follow others with inner strength and faith and conviction. Even if alpha males don't have the right title or right placement in the hierarchy, their confidence, their inner strength, and their trust in themselves make them natural magnets for those around them.

It's not uncommon for an alpha male to be actually the shots and telling the "acknowledged" leader what to do. Real alpha males are more than comfortable with this. They are also more than comfortable with calling the shots from behind the scenes. After all, they're so confident that they're not out to hog the spotlight or hog the credit. They're beyond that.

Finally, alpha males know that leadership influence is earned. They work for it. You don't get it just because you show up with a name tag with "MANAGER" printed on it, and it doesn't mean people will automatically respect you.

Influence is earned by one good decision at a time, day by day. Alpha males lead by example and by the strength of their character and how people perceive it.

9. Alpha males find joy in their journey.

I've touched on this before, but one of the biggest delusions that people have about their lives is that at a certain point, they're just done. They're not necessarily complete, but they've gotten as far as they can. They've accomplished what they have been put on this earth to do, and they are content with not striving for more.

It's a terrible mindset, and the worst form of self-deception ever.

Life is a LIFELONG journey.

Your goals aren't the end all be all, because once you've reached them... you should be suddenly unfulfilled again and reaching for the next ones. This is all part of the journey, and it's an endless pursuit of happiness. The moment you stop moving this way, well... that's called **settling**, no matter how high you have climbed.

Alpha males know the futility of this. This is why they stand apart from the rest. They seek to complete themselves, with the never-ending journey and process being an essential aspect of that.

Alpha males understand that life is a process. It's a life of constant change and constant becoming, where the only constant is change itself.

Instead of feeling that this is some sort of cosmic treadmill that really leads nowhere, instead they gain their fulfillment from it because they are at peace with the process and journey.

They're not looking at a final product. They're not looking at final destination. Instead, they're looking to find their happiness in the here and now throughout that process and journey. They're destined to feel slightly incomplete and not whole for their entire lives, but progress and the journey is more valuable than that.

In this day and age, it's very easy for people to define themselves based on what they do for living, who their parents are, what their experiences are, and other external factors.

The reality is that you aren't your job. You aren't your parents. You aren't your college degree or post-graduate degree. You aren't your income or net worth level. You aren't your experiences. You aren't any of those things. Instead, you are beyond and more than those things.

In our day and age, we are programmed to believe that our circumstances define us. That we can only be happy of certain things outside of us, line up, and fall into place. If you believe that lie, you will never be happy. Strive to be more than that, and find the joy in the journey to becoming more.

Of course, realizing that the journey is meant to be enjoyed isn't always enough to motivate us to that point. As with many things, self-completion is typically fueled by an **intimate passion for life**.

Alpha males have a passion for life because they understand that they are the creators of their own journeys and ultimately destiny. This is amazingly empowering, and means that their destinies are only limited by their sense of possibility.

Whichever journey the alpha male takes leads to a truly lived life because that's what they believe in.

A truly lived life means that you don't live for the future. You live day to day. You enjoy each day's victory, although, deep down, you have a general direction as to future goals. You celebrate the moment. This enables alpha males to live a life without fear, shame, guilt, and regret.

Alpha males believe in passion and that passion is manifested in the power of their dreams. They know that there is more to life than money, social status, or outward appearances.

Life is all about starting with nothing and building something. It's all about the process and journey. It is never about destination. Life is all about finding your own path. It is not something you attain. It's something you need to figure out for yourself.

And that's precisely what makes life's journeys so rewarding and worthy of focus.

10. Alpha males don't mind taking the road less traveled.

For all of the mystique surrounding Steve Jobs, the mercurial founder of Apple, he was called many things in his past.

A bum. A hippie. An **asshole**. The guy with terrible body odor. The guy who got kicked out of his own company.

This all fell on deaf ears to him.

He had a singular focus that made him indifferent to what people thought about him, and marched to the beat of his unique own drummer.

These days, it's fashionable to look up to Steve Jobs and his successes with Apple, but his life story contains another important lesson.

If you want to live your life to its fullest potential, and as the authentic version of yourself, here's a simple truth. You can't be afraid to be called weird, peculiar, smelly, or crazy. You can't be bothered to fall in line with other people's expectations and limits on you.

You can't be afraid to put yourself in uncomfortable and awkward situations where you stand against conventional wisdom or even conventional morality.

It's a difficult path to think about… because most people are slaves of the herd mentality. They want to be like everyone else because they don't want to be forsaken or neglected. Herd mentality is all about fear. It's all about people being afraid of being left out.

But if you keep your ideas firmly within the box of conventional wisdom and what people are never surprised or impressed by, you're just suppressing your full potential and imagination.

Each and every genius in their own time was regarded as insane, and never truly recognized for their innovation and full value. These geniuses dared to look beyond conventional wisdom, and were so focused on their ideas that they didn't care that people refused to believe them or even called them crazy.

The pressure of conventional wisdom defeats creativity and stunts intellectual curiosity. If you're forced to operate within the tight confines of "just because that's how it is" then what kind of life are you going to live?

If Christopher Columbus and others bought into the lie that the world is flat and didn't question it, when would the New World have been discovered? How far back would western civilization be set?

We've addressed and gotten past the big reason that people don't blaze their own paths and think and act outside of conventional wisdom – fear.

So what about you?

You're special, and unique. You have the capacity to act and think beyond conventional wisdom, and no fear of leaving the herd should ever hold you back from going where you want.

Life is 100% what you make of it and you can live it completely on your own terms. Explore your interests, no matter or outlandish or unconventional. Become driven by your curiosity, a sense of possibility, and be motivated by the power of your dreams. Taking your own path doesn't just apply to your career and work – it should influence exactly how you spend every minute of your time with hobbies and interests as well.

Naysayers and people that don't necessarily support what you're doing? Deadweight, jealous people that don't have the courage to do what you're doing. They'll call you crazy and stupid because it reflects their own insecurities surrounding belonging and being accepted.

An alpha male lives life on his own terms, and doesn't mind taking the road less traveled. He is intentional about his activities and direction, even if the end goal is not always clear.

It's the fact that he has created his own goals and paths that makes him a true alpha male.

11. Alpha males are self-reliant and independent.

When people talk about success, it is inevitable for the discussion to skew towards the end results and fruits of that success.

The BMWs, big houses, expensive watches, luxurious meals, and lavish vacations.

Lost within that is all of the hard work and difficult process it took to get to that point. But the process to success isn't just about the entrepreneur taking the steps of starting a company, taking some risks, hedging failure, and finally succeeding in the end.

The true indicator of success is the mindset and approach that they have in their daily lives and how intentional about everything they are. So if you want to know why alpha males are so damn successful, look at the root causes – their independent and self-reliant "get shit done" mindsets.

Alpha males are independent and are comfortable relying solely upon themselves. They know this is the smartest option, as in the end only they will have themselves as their #1 priority.

They understand that depending on the efforts of other people ultimately weakens and lowers their value, as they will spend a lot of time waiting for others to get their act together. They won't be known as value providers, and eventually they'll become known as anchors and burdens. It also weakens their own resolve for independence and gives them the habit of letting others take the lead.

Alpha males just make it happen and become the wind behind the sails of everyone they meet. They just get up and do the damn thing. They act, they measure success, they make changes, and then do it all over again until it's just right. This is what creates progress and ultimate success.

This is a cycle of confidence building, as with each success the alpha male experiences, the more confident they will be going into their next venture. All it takes is one success to kickstart your infectious confidence and become a proudly independent person.

Most importantly, alpha males don't blame anyone else for their failures. They recognize that this is part of being self-reliant and independent, and take full ownership of their lives for better or worse. They aren't too proud to accept help, but never expect or depend on it.

When you blame other people, you are essentially handing over the ability to change the outcomes of your life to other people. If the blame lies in other people's hands, then ultimately the power is in their hands too. This of course leaves you powerless and unable to transition into the alpha male mentality.

Alpha males aren't beholden to anyone. They don't live their lives craving for the affirmation or appreciation of others. Approval of others isn't a priority to the independent alpha male, and likewise they don't wait around to give others approval. They just make things happen.

None of this means that alpha males eschew other people or don't get along with them in favor of that solitary log cabin. There's simply a stark difference between goodwill and friendship… and dependency. Unfortunately, all too often people blur the lines between those two concepts. The lines are just too easy to cross when you get along with someone.

You exist by yourself as a strong, independent alpha male island. Your existence is complete by yourself, and you don't need anyone or anything to make your day worth living. If you fall into that kind of thinking with your friends or girlfriend, you have just lost your independence and become their slave.

Dependency is the opiate of the lesser man, and you are beyond that.

12. Alpha males respect themselves enough to be in great shape.

Everything about you reflects your inner character, you values and your priorities.

Your clothes, your haircut, how you interact with others, and even how you walk. There are no ifs, ands, or buts here.

Most importantly, your physical fitness reflects who you really are inside. Why is this important? Because it's what people will judge you on immediately.

If you're not in great shape and don't take care of yourself, it's a reflection of your values and priorities.

They aren't on yourself, your health, or pride in yourself. Alpha males understand this intimately, so take care of themselves with pride and care. It reflects how much they respect themselves inside and out.

Not being in a great shape is a weakness of character. Your body is your temple, and you only get one. Treat it well and it will treat you well.

Everything is tied together in the alpha male: body, mind, emotions, spiritual well-being, and soul. They aren't separable, or dissectible. They function together as one, and if there is one weak link, then it risks your entire well-being. Most of what I've spoken about in this book has been towards the emotional mindsets, but that doesn't mean that the body is any less important.

Your self-worth is shown in your appearance. It shows how much you love and respect yourself. How can you expect other people to love and respect you when your health choices manifest a disrespect and lack of love for yourself? Other people can only love you as much as you love and respect yourself.

As much as we'd like to pretend that this isn't the case, we live in a shallow world that runs on split-second judgments and preconceived notions.

Just like your physical shape, your grooming and hygiene reflects your values. The ability to do something continuously and consistently every single days reflects an inner strength and discipline.

Discipline is about doing things that aren't always convenient, and that you might even just hate. But doing these things and building up a tolerance and willpower is extremely valuable and helps you lay the groundwork for a more powerful, effective, and happier life.

Think about where discipline adds value to your life – business, school, fitness, social skills, romance, friendship… the list is endless. Alpha males have the utmost of discipline regarding their lives, and this shows in their hygiene and grooming. Let it begin there and carry over to the rest of your life.

Guess where else the alpha male's discipline and focus are reflected? His diet.

Alpha males know that addiction takes many forms, and just because you are healthy in disregarding smoking or drugs doesn't mean that you're free from addiction – to fatty foods.

Alpha males control their diet and fight temptations and urges to regularly become a glutton. They are all about moderation and balance.

Alpha males are focused on fighting urges because they know that any sort of imbalance makes them lose control over their own lives, which they have fought tough to maintain discipline and focus over. If you're a slave to a cigarette or donut, you have no control over a substantial part of your life and what drives you on a daily basis.

At the root, not treating your body like a temple is internal weakness, and alpha males are all about internal strength that is infectious and spreads outwards.

13. Alpha males embrace role models.

I make no secret of the fact that I still idolize Will Smith's Fresh Prince character from the similarly named television show.

To me, he's everything that a charming, alpha male should be. He says what he wants, is amazingly likeable, is comfortable being at the center of the room, is confident to the point of being arrogant, and most of all he is hilarious. His mannerisms with women are also off the charts.

Just my conception, of course.

When I was first starting to diligently grow my own alpha male identity and break out of my shell, he was an important concept for me. Since he embodied many of the things I wanted, I was able to grow, sometimes in a forced and artificial way, closer to my personal ideal simply by asking myself one question.

What would the Fresh Prince do?

It's a powerful question to ask yourself for a reasons.

First, it takes the focus off the situation at hand that you might not be comfortable in.

Asking yourself a question about how someone else would act takes the pressure off of asking how you yourself should act. It's always easier to observe and give advice to other people (hello, relationships), and it's no different here. Viewing things through an objective, relatively impersonal perspective and frame of someone else will allow you to analyze the social situation that you are in, and calibrate your next moves.

Second, it allows you to actually develop your alpha male identity to the end goal that you want.

Every time you ask yourself this question, your reaction and justification will become that much easier until it is second nature. There's no awkward fumbling about and analyzing situations in hindsight – you will essentially be able to condition yourself in the heat of the moment to act how you want and make your actions as a reflex.

Third, simply having a role model (or 3) in mind allows you to analyze what traits you actually value and want to develop.

For instance, perhaps you want to develop more confidence and being more outspoken in social situations. In that case, you might ask yourself what someone like Robert Downey Jr. would do. For another trait you want to develop, for example a razor sharp sense of wit and humor, perhaps you could ask yourself what Conan O'Brien would do.

Everyone has different strengths and weaknesses, and has a different conception of how they want to be perceived. Not everyone fits the blatantly outgoing mold of being alpha, and that's fine.

Other people that tend to resonate with others in terms of wanting to emulate: Tyler Durden, Don Draper, Charles Zavier, Jack Donaghy, Ari Gold, John Wayne… the list goes on. It's about choosing someone that excels in areas that you feel like you don't, and embodying them from time to time to create lasting habits.

Fourth, thinking about what someone would do is like wearing a mask at first. As any trick or treater can attest to, masks empower us and allow us to say and think things that we wouldn't dare to otherwise. In a sense, this becomes a safe place for you to retreat you when you are in an unfamiliar social situation.

This principle is simply about introspection – recognizing your faults and shortcomings honestly, and implementing a quick mental fix to help you develop your skills into a level of alpha male.

14. Alpha males embrace vulnerability.

People simply eat up the fact that I was a near-obese adolescent. Why?

Vulnerability – arguably, the most supreme and evolved form of confidence. If confidence itself is a game-changer, consider vulnerability re-writing the rules of the game itself.

Vulnerability isn't a sob story or being a sensitive push over. When I refer to vulnerability, I mean expressing yourself without shame or apology, embracing opposition and rejection by others, and willing to take risks for your beliefs and values.

It's the principle of recognizing who you are and what you stand for, and being amazingly comfortable with it. When you're comfortable with yourself, others become comfortable with you too, and it has a certain way of putting people at ease.

Alpha males possess this in spades. Learn it and love it.

Vulnerability draws others to you, and instantly makes you attractive in the sense that you are so comfortable with yourself that you can express yourself without caring about the reaction from others. It shows a sense of proactivity and introspection, as you have principles and stances based on your beliefs. What is more alpha than that?

Most of all, vulnerability allows you to display supreme confidence in yourself, whether you really feel that way or not. Putting yourself out there is an admirable act, and most people will be in awe and envious of you instead of putting any judgment on you like you might think.

When the alpha males truly allows vulnerability and puts a certain amount of judging power into the hands of other people, it's a powerful gesture. He doesn't have to step on anyone to maintain his confidence, and can even find the humor in his flaws and judgments that other people impose on him. People, not just women, tend to gravitate towards those that are straightforward and aren't attempting to be something they are not. They'll know what they are getting, and will in turn open up to you in a way that you ever thought possible.

So back to my opening statement for this chapter – why do women love the fact that I was a Michelin baby and adolescent?

It's a fact that I find hilarious about myself. Many people can often relate to it. It disarms people and shows that I don't take myself that seriously. It shows that I have no issues letting chinks like that slide, and that I don't care if they tend to diminish my overall image. Most of all, I'm confident enough in myself to turn something potentially embarrassing into a uniquely vulnerable connecting point.

I am who I am, and you can accept me or not. And more often than not, after I share it, I get back something that they are insecure or that makes them vulnerable, and an instant deep bond is created.

Let's look at the other side:

If I was to be ashamed of this small fact, how would it reflect on the rest of my self-image and how others could deal with it? They would know that it's a sore spot, and would have to avoid it altogether. Tensions rise, and must be diverted.

An alpha male's ability to be the attractive man that a woman desires is directly proportional to how vulnerable he is willing to make himself. Vulnerability is what communicates a man's desires, and if they are actually expressed.

The flip side, of course, is the passive beta male who doesn't freely express his opinion, quite possibly is a pushover, and seeks to please people instead of live his own life.

He's simply not willing to take the leap of attempting to assert himself or open himself up to judgment in any way.

Vulnerability is an often overlooked element of attraction and self-esteem. Of course, even though I've told you how people subconsciously embrace the presence of vulnerability and impart a slew of positive adjectives to it, it doesn't mean that you won't have your mental blocks preventing you from immediately telling people your business.

Vulnerability is a process, but is one well-worthy of conquering as the pinnacle of alpha male confidence.

15. The 28 day Alpha Male Kickstart Plan.

We know that there a ton of misconceptions about the modern alpha male. He's distant and emotionless. He's an ass to women. He's like James Bond. He's an incredibly extrovert that is always at the center of the party.

While some of these are actually positive perceptions, it doesn't mean that the expectations they place on men aren't still damaging.

The most damaging misconception is that the alpha male was simply born that way, and you either have it or you don't. All or nothing. This of course is one of the excuses that people give themselves when faced with the challenge of putting in the work to improve themselves. These are all cop outs and excuses to mask a fear of rejection or failure.

It's a complete and utter lie, a false dichotomy.

Just like with everything else in life, you can become whatever you want to be. We are all given the gift of self-invention. We create our own selves and identity and shouldn't squander the privilege we have to do that. We can become what they focus on.

To accept anything less is to settle for mediocrity and is a defeatist attitude.

Becoming a true alpha male is no different from becoming a lawyer, doctor, teacher… a great father, a good manager, or a better runner. It's something you become through a process of improvement and intentional choices intended to grow yourself in a particular direction.

Everyone starts somewhere, but it's always a choice to become something – nothing is off limits or unattainable to the alpha male.

You made a choice by buying this book. Let's continue with these positive, life-changing choices with my 28 day Alpha Male Kickstart Plan below. It's by no means exhaustive, but it outlines a holistic overview of all aspects of the life that the alpha male has mastery over, and seeks to continually improve upon.

The Alpha Body: Day 1-7

This 28 day Kickstart starts with your body. This is the easiest aspect to change, and likely where you'll see the most immediate benefits. Your body is easy to manipulate in terms of habits and rituals, and pave the way for your inner changes to begin and take hold.

Devote the first 7 days to this aspect.

Get your diet in check, any diet regimen will do as long as it is one you can stick with consistently.

This means stopping with the compulsive eating, and finding out exactly how many calories you need to hit your target weight, whether it's a surplus or deficit. Get your fiber, vegetables, proteins, and don't neglect your fats. Stop snacking and drink less soda. Consider a fasting schedule, and cut down on your caffeine.

Just do it. You're above your temptations and urges – take control of them. What excuses do you really have?

Test your discipline by sticking to the diet guidelines you meet, no matter what. Easier said than done of course, but this is crucial. A great body speaks to far more than simply eating the right things – it speaks to the strength of character and disciplined required to maintain and build your alpha male body.

Next of course, you hit the damn gym. Or start doing pushups and situps on a regular schedule. It doesn't matter what you choose to do, just that you do it constantly and consistently. Test your discipline here too – it will carry focus over to the rest of your life and help your time management as well. Stick to your schedule, and prioritize yourself over social gatherings and other shit for the meantime. If you don't think you have time for this aspect, you're dead wrong Pushups and situps take 10 minutes a day, and you need to sorely re-examine your priorities.

Hygiene routines? I hope you don't need to kickstart these.

Physical changes and routines are key that they impart focus, discipline, and strength. Weak men deviate from their schedules and don't prioritize themselves. Alpha males stay strong in the face of difficult challenges, and honor themselves by conquering what is in front of them.

An added bonus is the surge of confidence that physical improvements will do to your psyche.

The Alpha Mind: Day 8-14

Starting with day 8, we turn our attention to your mindset and approach towards life. We keep exercising the discipline and strength that we found in days 1-7, but gradually introduce practices that impact the mind here.

Embrace this simple concept: master your mindset and your master your destiny.

Your outer world is really a reflection of your inner world. If you're unhappy, it's because you chose to be unhappy. That's the power of the mind.

It's not something we think about, or are even aware of. Most people are like zombies that are just basically floating from day to day, and they're being swept by all sorts of emotions that they think are out of their control.

It's another lie.

If you are conscious and deliberate about the thoughts that you choose, you can master your happiness and outcomes. One of the best ways to do this is to practice meditation or mindfulness daily. Learn some key mental control practices like learning to forgive, learning not to judge your thoughts, and learning to always maintain control of your thoughts.

Let's face it. All sorts of negative mental pictures enter our minds every single day. However, it is up to us to determine what kind of emotional meaning those mental pictures have.

Take control of this process.

I know this is not very easy but the more you try it, the better you get at it. Eventually, you can attain such a high degree of control over the emotional meaning of your thoughts that this can lead to greater control and mastery over your actions and ultimately your life.

<u>Alpha Emotions: Day 15-21</u>

Now that we have a strong foundation with the mental and physical elements of the quintessential alpha male, we turn to your emotions.

This might be the most difficult part of the whole process because of how we men are socialized and conditioned in western society (be strong, stoic, show no emotion, emotion is weakness, just "man up", and so on) but it is key to embracing your new alpha male identity.

Think closely each day about what has come across your path, and what has made you feel emotion. Strip away any form of judgment on yourself, and just admit to yourself what impacts you without any of the defense mechanisms we always use.

Consider starting a journal to track your emotions and open yourself up to vulnerability. Learn how you can improve your emotional intelligence and exactly why you feel the way that you do on a daily basis.

Question everything in your life. Are you happy? Do you even know what happiness feels like? What makes you happy on a daily basis? What should you be prioritizing in your life that you aren't?

Focus on those and write a plan on how to be happier on a day to day basis based on your personal definition of happiness... and NO ONE ELSE'S.

To paraphrase John Lennon, the real job of a human being is ultimately to be happy. If you're not being happy, and you're not working towards achieving a state of happiness, you're doing it wrong. Learn to love yourself and happiness.

What are you even doing?

Alpha Meaning: Day 22-28

Let's face it. Most people just trudge through their lives. They're driven by sex, food, social status, or money.

Nowhere in there is what matters the most – happiness, as we discussed earlier... and finding meaning and fulfillment in their lives. This is the apex of happiness.

Unfortunately, few people reach this level because they're so preoccupied with just paying the rent, making it to the next day, finding a love partner. And it's just not an easy question to ask yourself without knowing yourself intimately well.

Ask yourself what your destiny is. What makes you happy. What you find meaning in. What you want to dedicate your time to. What your personal meaning might be. What your passions are. What you offer the world others do not. What takes advantage of your strengths. What fulfills you. What you see yourself doing in 10 years. What you would do if money weren't important. What besides work do you want to pursue, and are passionate about?

Alpha males don't flounder around through their lives just hoping to get lucky and find their passion and meaning randomly. When alpha males comprehend the power of their dreams and goals, they allow that power to push them forward.

Here's a simple exercise to help you answer all of those questions I posed above.

Start with your longterm goals, I'm talking 20 years in the future. Who do you want to be, and where? Work backwards through all the steps needed to reach that point until you reach your present day status quo.

If you think hard enough about this and are realistic about the goals you have, you should end up with a nice plan of action for the next year, next 5 years, and ultimately for the rest of your future. Break your objectives into smaller goals, and break those into daily to-do lists. Stick to your timeline. Don't let your work define you.

This is how you work to a meaning-centered existence.

Conclusion

As you can see, becoming the modern alpha male is no small feat. But through this book, you should be able to see exactly why the alpha male is an ideal that so many men want to attain.

They are strong, confident, self-assured, focused, lead, and above all, love themselves. There are many themes that you can focus on and even spend years on, but loving and respecting yourself and your capability for strength should be your first priority. From that flows everything that the modern alpha male stands for and is always recognized for.

No one ever said that developing yourself, especially in ways that might be counterintuitive or contrary to your nature, would be easy. But that's the rub, isn't it? Nothing worthwhile in this life ever comes easy. The more you work and push your comfort zones, the greater the satisfaction you'll receive when one of your friends greets you with an amazingly positive "You've changed!"

The modern alpha male – he's a compendium of traits I believe to be holistically balanced and ready for battle. You have all the tools and knowledge at your disposal, so now it's up to you to seek your own modern alpha male destiny.

Best of luck.

Sincerely,

Patrick King
Dating and Social Skills Coach
www.PatrickKingConsulting.com

P.S. If you enjoyed this book, please don't be shy and drop me a line, leave a review, or both! I love reading feedback, and reviews are the lifeblood of Kindle books, so they are always welcome and greatly appreciated.

Other books by Patrick King include:

CHATTER: Small Talk, Charisma, and How to Talk to Anyone http://www.amazon.com/dp/B00J5HH2Y6

Charm Her Socks Off: Creating Chemistry from Thin Air http://www.amazon.com/dp/B00IEO688W

Why Women Love Jerks: Realizing the Best Version of Yourself to Effortlessly Attract Women
http://www.amazon.com/dp/B00KLPXNI0

Cheat sheet

1. An alpha male prioritizes personal growth and doesn't settle for the status quo. He seeks any opportunity to keep growing himself and makes a concerted effort to improve every aspect about himself.

2. An alpha male has supreme confidence and security in himself. He is secure enough to blaze his own path because he knows that to do anything less is to settle for mediocrity.

3. An alpha male is always composed and in control of the situation. He knows that he cannot control life circumstances, but he can control his emotions and reactions, and thus stays even-keeled.

4. An alpha male looks his fears in the eye and laughs at them. It's not always direct courage that inspires an alpha male to conquer fears, being goal-oriented and focused will also destroy fears.

5. An alpha male assumes responsibility. He doesn't shy away from all consequences of his actions and word, whether they are positive or negative.

6. An alpha male's self-knowledge inspires true confidence. He is intimately aware of his own strengths and weaknesses and accepts them confidently.

7. An alpha male gives women the respect they deserve. He knows that women are human beings as well to be cherished, and are not just objects for their own amusement.

8. An alpha male is a natural leader because of how he treats others. He inspires infectious confidence by how much positivity he reflects to those he leads, in work and otherwise.

9. An alpha male finds joy in his journey. Goals and accomplishments are important but the learning of the journey is arguably more valuable and enjoyable than the end point.

10. An alpha male doesn't mind taking the road less traveled. He doesn't let anyone else's opinions influence how he spends his time and creates his goals by himself.

11. Alpha males are self-reliant and independent. He knows that putting responsibility or blame in the hands of someone else means a perpetual loss of independence and determination of destiny.

12. Alpha Males Respect Themselves Enough to be in Great Shape. He respects his one body for the temple that it is and knows that his physical fitness is a large part of his self-worth.

13. Embrace your alpha role model. He utilizes role models intelligently to focus his efforts on development and follow a lead.

14. An alpha male embraces vulnerability. He knows that vulnerability is the ultimate form of confidence and draws people to him.

15. The 28 day Alpha Male Kickstart Plan. You'll just have to read the entire Kickstart Plan, because there's no use in reducing an already reduced outline ☺.